Winner of the 2018
AGO/Marilyn Mason Award in Organ Composition

The AGO/Marilyn Mason Award in Organ Composition is held every two years. Originally known as the AGO/Holtkamp Award, the competition began in partnership with the Holtkamp Organ Company in 1984. In 2012, Marilyn Mason became the new sponsor. The winner of this competition receives a $2,000 prize, publication of the piece by Hinshaw Music Inc., or The H. T. FitzSimons Company, both imprints within the Fred Bock Publishing Group, and a world premiere performance at the AGO National Convention. The present procedure is to call for proposals for the commission of an organ solo work. Rather than prescribed criteria, the competition encourages proposals that reflect a composer's particular strengths and interests. A finished piece may also be submitted if it fills the criteria of the guidelines. This competition is biennial and calls for a work for organ solo; the specific requirements vary each year the competition is held.

Table of Contents

Artist Statement

My work as a composer combines the traditional and non-traditional in surprising ways. I present the listener with a conservative genre, a classic form, or a familiar "antique," a pre-existing composition from the canon of Western art music. This material is then dramatically reworked, incorporating elements from both art music and popular music of the 20th century. The result is a new composition, coherent in its own right, but containing an unlikely combination of materials.

In the organ work "Re-Formations (after Bach)," my source material is three chorale preludes for organ by the 18th Century master. These are paired with material not typically associated with Baroque organ music: early modernism, and 20th century popular music and dance styles. The chorale tunes and Bach's figurations remain recognizable, but they are not merely quoted or arranged. They are "re-formed" to become elements within the themes and structures of three new movements.

The results may strike the listener as peculiar, fascinating, intense, or even hilarious. Bach's famous pedal line of "In Thee Is Gladness" becomes a trumpet solo, while the new pedal line invokes a walking bass pattern. The rapid figurations in "Where Shall I Flee?" are elongated enormously to become a slow-drag blues melody, while its chorale tune is compacted and developed into material reminiscent of silent-film-era theater organ music. "Beloved, One and All, Rejoice!" reorganizes the chorale phrases into a Sonata-Allegro form, with Bach's setting presented in the rhythms of a hip-hop dance.

What does hip-hop have to do with Sonata-Allegro form? Or a German chorale with silent movie music? Very little, and this is precisely the point. Finding a compelling way to bring together disparate elements is the hallmark of my work.

Performance Notes

"Re-Formations (after Bach)" presents material in the musical styles of different time periods and cultures. Contrasting registrations as well as contrasting rhythmic approaches will help to invoke these different styles.

For example, some of the suggested registrations reflect the world of Bach, like the opening registration of the first movement, with its "Werkprinzip" Great principal chorus and bright flue stops on the Choir (with the Choir acting like a Rückpositiv). Other suggested registrations, however, are decidedly not Baroque, like the symphonic-organ-style registration at the beginning of the second movement, with its early 20th century aesthetic of multiple 8' stops.

Similarly, some rhythms are from the world of art music and others are from the world of popular music. Specifically, the rhythms notated as triplets in the first and third movements indicate "swing" rhythms. As is typical in folk, jazz, and other popular music styles, swing rhythms needn't fit into exact triplet measurements, but should have a relaxed "bounce." ("Notes inégale" is a similar idea from the organ world.) However, this applies only to the rhythms notated as triplets; all other rhythms are standard (or "straight").

Tempo and articulation should be guided to some degree by the acoustics of the room in order for both the Baroque and the popular-music idioms to speak clearly. For example, the "Hip-hop shuffle" triplet rhythms of the last movement could be articulated in various ways (everything short, sixteenths phrased into short eighths, etc.) in order to produce the rhythmic vitality of a hip-hop dance. In the first movement, breath marks indicate a lift between phrases (while maintaining a steady beat – not a distortion of tempo), and throughout the score, notes marked with a "mezzo-staccato" (̣̄) are held somewhat less than full value (but not short like a staccato). Again, the degree of lift or space between notes can be adjusted based on acoustics and the specific instrument.

Because of their multi-stylistic nature, the pieces are most ideally suited to an eclectic 3-manual or 4-manual organ in a medium acoustic. Registrations shown in parenthesis are optional additions which the performer may add if available or if needed for balance between manuals; there are also optional additions suggested if a 4th manual is available. On smaller or less eclectic instruments, consideration should be given to the distinguishing characteristics of the suggested registrations when making adaptations. Here are some specific registration guidelines for each movement:

In Thee Is Gladness

The dialogue between the Great and Choir (mm. 3-18) should feature two distinct timbres, even as stops are gradually added to both, with the Great being more warm and full, and the Choir being more bright and sparkling. (The manuals may be reversed if it facilitates producing this effect.)

At m. 23, the Swell and Great registrations should be contrasting but equally present. If the Swell reeds are not big enough to balance the Great principal chorus, solo reeds may be used; make sure each manual can be heard as its own separate layer.

Where Shall I Flee?

Many of the registrations in this movement are inspired by early 20th century symphonic and theater organs. The Great registration in m. 3 should be warm and thick, with the Diapason sound predominating.

In m. 13, a fast tremulant on the Swell is desirable, while the Choir registration should be thin, nasal, and pungent, like a saxophone section.

In m. 32, the Swell Vox Humana with Tremulant should be heard equally with the Choir registration; if the Vox Humana is too soft, a Sw. to Sw. 4' coupler may be used. If none of these options are available, play the ossia line with its alternative registration and tremolo markings.

Beloved, One and All, Rejoice!

The Choir "Cromorne + higher-pitched flue stops" registration at the beginning (and recurring throughout the movement) is meant to imitate the twang of an electric guitar; the stops used should be bright, reedy and piquant, and must articulate the rhythmic figuration clearly. For example, a very smooth Clarinet stop would not function well here, but a "barking" Regal would be ideal. Use the Octave and Quint or other higher pitched flue stops as needed to produce this effect.

In mm. 49 and 51, this same Choir registration should contrast with the lush, symphonic-organ-inspired Great registration, with humorous effect. On larger organs, more layers of Strings and Célestes may be added to the Great.

In m. 54, the 4' flue stop on the Great needs to be prominent enough to mask the "disappearance" of the sound of the Sw. to Gt. 4' on the high "D" (which is out of register). Alternatively, if a 4' String and Céleste pair is available on the Swell, it can be used along with an Octave 4' in lieu of the Sw. to Gt. 4' coupler.

In mm. 73-75, the final chorale phrase of BWV 734 is quoted directly, and the registration should sound traditionally German Baroque. However, to facilitate the abrupt transitions into and out of this passage, the Pedal line is notated an octave lower than in Bach's original, and the manual parts are notated an octave higher. In order to correct for this octave displacement and produce a realization standard to the works of Bach, the registrations for the manuals are 16'-based (sounding "down an octave" to match the original) and the Pedal line couples a 4' reed stop with a 4' coupler (sounding "up an octave" to match the original). If this solution is unavailable, try to get as close as possible to a traditional registration; this may involve playing one of the lines in a different octave than notated. (Refer to BWV 734 for clarification.)

In the final two measures, the use of Swell sub and super couplers (even with full Swell containing 16') enables a more dramatic fp, crescendo, and final accent, creating a "32' sound" in the manuals.

Mark Kurtz is a composer, pianist, organist, and music director. Originally from North Dakota, he has lived and worked in Omaha since 2000. He has become known for being adept in an unusually broad spectrum of genres, including both art music and popular music. A sought-after performer and inventive creator, his work can be found in concert halls, churches, theaters, cabarets, and convention centers.

His colorful, multi-stylistic compositions have been performed at GALA international choral festivals (Miami in 2008 and Montréal in 2004), regional conventions (Nebraska Choral Directors Association in 2016 and the American Guild of Organists – Southeast - in 2011), many churches and community choruses from Washington, D.C. (2014 and 2012) to St. Paul, MN (2017) to Los Altos, CA (2006), and in his local vicinity of Omaha by organizations like Gallup (2017 and 2016), Circle Theater (2017), Résonance (2016), the American Guild of Organists (hymn festivals 2016 and 2015), Horizons of Faith (2011), and the River City Mixed Chorus (2014, 2008, and 2007). A choral piece was featured on the radio broadcast "Going Beyond Words." (2012)

Besides being the music director at First United Methodist Church (Omaha) and Associate Director and Collaborative Pianist for Résonance (a professional choral ensemble), he frequently works with the Omaha Symphony (as rehearsal pianist and substitute pianist/organist for concerts), and has performed chamber music alongside symphony members. He frequently receives commissions for new work, from organizations such as the Willa Cather Foundation (2017), the Anti Defamation League (2012), Why Arts (2011), and the River City Mixed Chorus (2014 and 2008), as well as many churches and individuals, for example, poet Fred Zydek (2013) and Omaha Symphony members Craig and Mary Bircher (2012). He has received numerous scholastic, performance, and composition awards, most recently from the American Guild of Organists (2018 and 2011) and Omaha Entertainment and Arts (2011).

His teachers have included organist and early music specialist John Mueller at the North Carolina School of the Arts, composer/organist William Albright at the University of Michigan, and composer Dominik Argento at the University of Minnesota. Significant mentors in his career have been composer/organist Robert Hebble, composer Alex Lubet, and conductor/composer Ernest Richardson.

Re-Formations
(after Bach)

I. In Thee Is Gladness

Mark Kurtz

Sw. Viola 8', Voix Céleste 8', Flute 4'
Gt. Principals 16', 8', 4', 2'; Mixture
Ch. Gedackt 8' and bright 2'
Ped. Principals 16', 8'

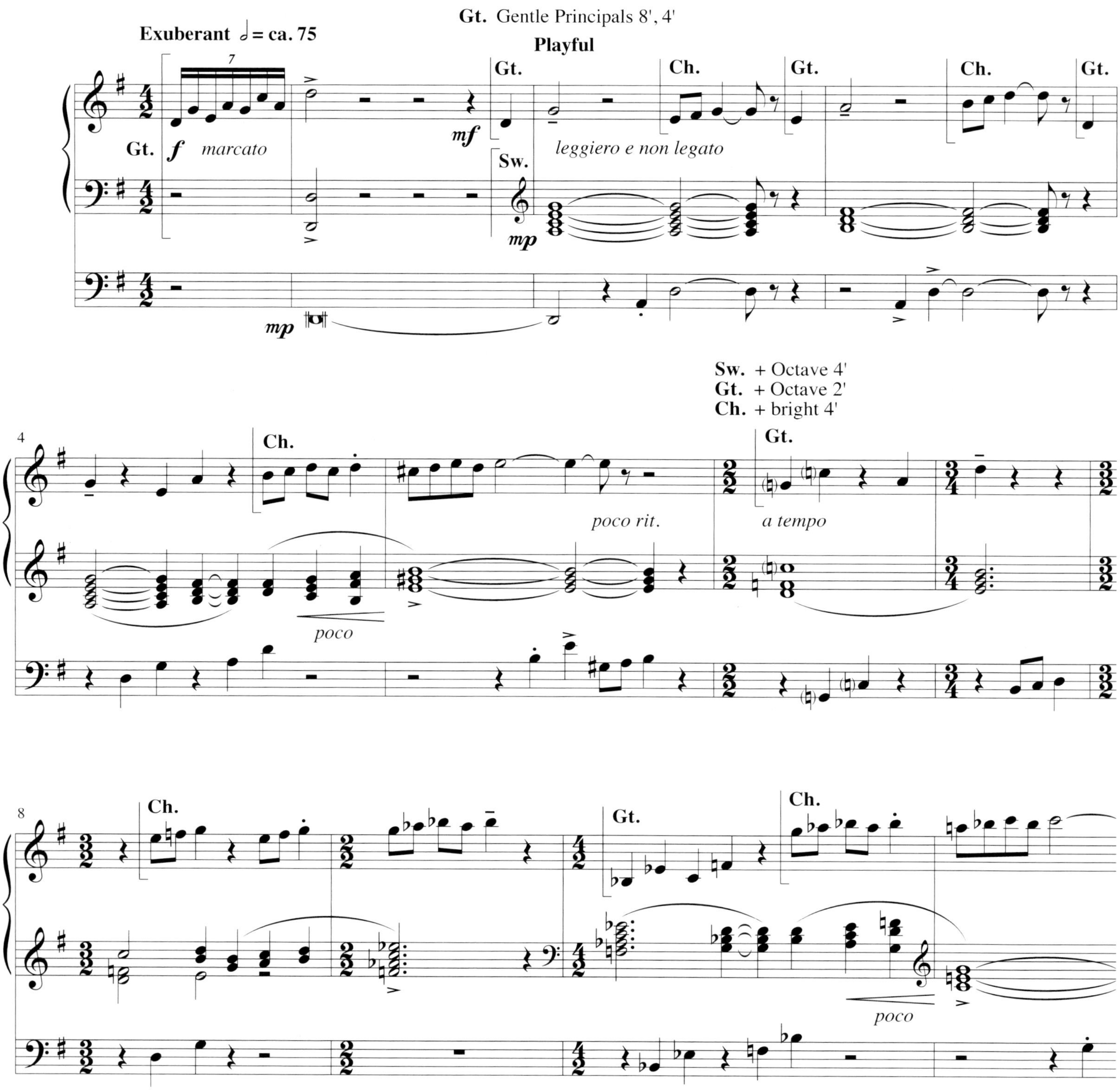

F0675

Sw. + Principals 8', 2'; Oboe 8'; - Voix Céleste 8'
Gt. + Principal 16', Quint 2-2/3', Trumpet 8' (and Terz 1-3/5')
Ch. Flutes 8', 4' and bright 1'
Ch. leggiero e non legato
Sw.
mf
piu legato
poco
Gt. f
Sw.
più f
Ch.
Gt.
poco
Sw. + Mixture
Gt. Principals 16', 8', 4', 2'; Mixture
Ch. Horizontal Trumpet 8'
Ped. Principals 16', 8', 4'; Mixture
Gt.
Sw.
f
ff poco a poco piu mosso
+ Sw. Trumpet 8'
Gt.
Exuberant = ca. 75; tempo guisto al fine
Triplets indicate swing rhythms; all other eighths straight
Sw. Reeds 8', 4' (or Solo)
Ped. + Principal 2'
Ch.
fff
poco tenuto
Gt.
sempre marcato
ff ("In Dir ist Freude")
Ch.
fff
Gt.
Sw.

Gt.
Sw.
Ch.
Sw. Principals 8', 4', 2'; Mixture; Trumpet 8'; (and Clarion 4')
(Sw. Clarion 4' off)

35
Sw.
mf
Gt.
ff
Sw. Reeds 8', 4'
(or Solo)
38
Sw.
Gt.
Ch.
fff
40
Gt.
ff
Sw.
Ch.
fff
Gt.
42
Gt.
ff
Sw.
Gt.
Sw.
Ch.
fff
Sw.

Sw. Principals 8', 4', 2'; Mixture; Trumpet 8' (and Clarion 4')
Gt. + Trumpet 8' (and Clarion 4')
45
Gt.
ff
Sw.
Sw. Principals 8', 4', 2'; Oboe 8'; Trumpet 8'
Gt. Principals 8', 4', 2'; Quint 2⅔'; Terz 1-3/5'; Trumpet 8'
Ch. Flutes 8', 4', 1⅓'
Ped. Principals 16', 8' (and 4')
47
mf
Sw.
Ch.
mf
Gt.
f
Ch.
49
Sw.
mf
Gt.
f
Ch.
mf
51
Gt.
f
molto marcato
Sw.
Gt. Trumpet 8' off
mf
poco a poco cresc.
marcato

Sw. Viola 8' and Voix Céleste 8' (and Diap, 8')
Gt. Diapason 8', Sw. to Gt. 8'
Ch. Flutes 8', 2'
Ped. Flutes 16', 8'

+ Sw. Octaves 4', 2'; Vox Humana 8'
Gt.
+ Gt. Octave 4'
66
Gt.
mp
mf lush
69
Ch. Flutes 8', 4'
mp
Ped. + Flutes 4', 2'
(or Ch. to Ped. 4')
Sw. Principals 8', 4'
Gt. Bourdon 16', Octave 2'
72
Ch.
p leggiero
Gt.
8va
75
8va
Sw.
Ch.

Gt. Principals 16', 8', 4', 2'; Mixture
Ch. Horizontal Trumpet 8'
Ped. Principals 16', 8', 4', 2'; Mixture
78
Gt.
ff
81
Ch.
fff
Sw. Principals 8', 4', 2'; Mixture; Trumpet 8'; Clarion 4'
83
Gt.
Sw.
mf
ff
fff
Ch.
poco a poco allarg.
85
Sw.
molto allarg.
Ch.
a tempo
con brio
Gt.
sffz
+ Ch. Bourdon 16'; Principals 8', 4', 2'
+ Sw. to Ch. 16', 8'
Ped. + ff Reeds 16', 8'

II. Where Shall I Flee?

Mark Kurtz

Sw. Flutes 8', 2'; Tremulant; **Sw.** to **Sw.** 16', 4'; **Sw.** Unison off
Gt. Open Diapason 8' and Trumpet 8' (plus Quintadena 8' and/or Flute 4')
(Opt. **Solo** English Horn 8' to **Gt.** 8')
Ch. Bright 4' flue stop
Ped. Principals or Flutes 16', 8'

Slow drag blues ♩. = 72-75; steady tempo throughout

10
Ch. Narrow String 8' and Flute 4' (and Nazard 2⅔')
13
Sw.
mp
legato
("Wo soll ich fliehen hin")
Ch.
mp
quasi string bass pizz.
Sw. Principals 8', 4', 2'; Sesquialtera II; Tremulant
16
Sw. Viola 8' and Voix Céleste 8'
Gt. Flute 4'
Ch. Open Flute 8'
19
Gt.
p

22
Sw.
p
Gt.
p
Ch.
mp
Sw. Diapason 8'; Flutes and Strings 8', 4'; Tremulant; Sw. to Sw. 16'
Gt. Principals 8', 4'
Ch. Cromorne 8'
25
Sw.
legato
mf
Ch.
mf
28
(Sw.)
Gt.
(bridge)
Sw. Vox Humana 8' with fast Tremulant (Opt. Sw. to Sw. 4')
Ch. Flutes 8', 2'
31
Ch.
mp
Sw.
mp
Ossia L.H.
(if Vox Humana and Tremulant is unavailable)
Gt. Bourdon 8', coupled with Sw. Flutes 8', 4'
Gt.
mp

Gt. Principals 8', 4', 2'
+ Ch. to Ch. 4'
+ Gt. Mixture; + Full Sw. to Gt. (box shut - no 16')
Gt.
mf
mf
Gt.
f
Ped. Principals 16', 8', 4'; Mixture
f
poco
Sw. Viola 8' and Voix Céleste 8'; Sw. to Sw. 4'
(Opt. plus Vox Humana 8' - no Tremulant)
Gt. Flutes 8', 4'
Ch. Salicional 8', Quintadena 8', Flute 4', Nazard 2⅔'
Ped. Principals or Flutes 16', 8'
ff
mp
poco
meno mosso
Ch.
mp
a tempo

46
Sw.
legato
p
mp
Sw. Flutes 8', 2'; Tremulant; Sw. to Sw. 16', 4'; Sw. Unison off
Gt. Flute 4'
Ch. Diapason 8'
49
Gt.
p
Ch.
Gt. Open Diapason 8' and Trumpet 8'
(plus Quintadena 8' and/or Flute 4')
(Opt. Solo English Horn 8' and Tuba 8' to Gt. 8')
53
Sw.
legato
poco rit.
Ped. Principals 16', 8', 4'
Sw. Principals 8', 4', 2'
57
Sw.
a tempo
f
Gt.
ff

Sw. Principal 4' off
Gt. Trumpet 8' off
Ped. Principal 4' off
60
(Solo Tuba 8' off)
Gt.
Sw.
63
Ch. Bright 4' flue stop
Gt.
Ch.
Gt.
65
Ch. Softest 4'
67
Sw. Diapason 8'
Sw.
rall.
Ch.
Sw.
Ped. Violons 32', 16'

III. Beloved, One and All, Rejoice!

Mark Kurtz

Sw. Principals 8', 4', 2'; Mixture; Trumpet 8' (box closed)
Gt. Bright Trumpet 8' (and Octave 4')
Ch. Incisively articulate Cromorne 8' or Regal 8', Octave 4' or 2', and Quint 2⅔' or 1⅓'
Ped. Principals 16', 8', 4', 2'

Sw. Bourdon 16'; Principals 8', 4', 2'; Mixture; Trumpet 8' (+ Bassoon 16' and/or Clarion 4')
Gt. Principals 16', 8', 4', 2'; Mixture; Trumpet 8'; **Sw.** to **Gt.** 8'
Ped. Principals 32', 16', 8', 4', 2'; Mixture; assertive Reeds 16', 8'; **Sw.** to **Ped.** 8'

Sw. to Gt. 8' off
Gt.
f
ff
Sw.
Gt.
Sw.
Gt.
Sw. Principals 8', 4', 2'; Strings 8', 4'; Voix Céleste 8'
Gt. Principals 8', 4', 2'
Ped. Principals 16', 8', 4'
Sw.
Gt.
Sw.
legato
mf
Gt.
marcato
Ch.
Sw.
sempre legato
poco

(Previous Registration)
Sw. Bourdon 16'; Principals 8', 4', 2'; Mixture; Trumpet 8' (plus Bassoon 16' and/or Clarion 4')
Gt. Principals 16', 8', 4', 2'; Mixture; Trumpet 8'; **Sw.** to **Gt.** 8'
Ped. Principals 32', 16', 8', 4', 2'; Mixture; assertive Reeds 16', 8'; **Sw.** to **Ped.** 8'

Sw.
Gt.
Sw.
Gt.
Gt. Principals 8', 4', 2'
Ch. Principals 8', 4', 2'
Ped. Principals 16', 8', 4'
Gt.
mf
Ch.
Sw. Viola 8' and Gemshorn 8' (Opt: coupled to Solo Viola 8')
Gt. Diapason 8'; Sw. to Gt. 8'
Ch. Cromorne or Regal 8', Octave 4' or 2', and Quint 2⅔' or 1⅓'
Ped. Principals, Flutes, and/or Strings 16', 8'
Sw. suave
mp
Gt. mf

Sw. + Diapason 8', Voix Céleste 8', and Sw. to Sw. 4'
Gt. + Salicional 8' and Sw. to Gt. 4'
(Opt.: Solo Viola 8' and Voix Céleste 8' to Gt. 8', 4')
Ped. + Flute 4'
48
Gt.
Sw.
Ch.
mf
Gt.
mf lush
51
Sw.
Ch.
with humor
Gt.
Gt. + Principals and/or Flutes 8', 4'
54
esp.
Gt. Diapason 8', Bourdon 8', Harmonic Flute 8', Salicional 8'
mf
motoric
58
Ch. marcato
mf
Ped. Flutes 16', 8', 4'
mf

Sw. Principals 8' , 4'
Gt. Principals 16', 8', 4'

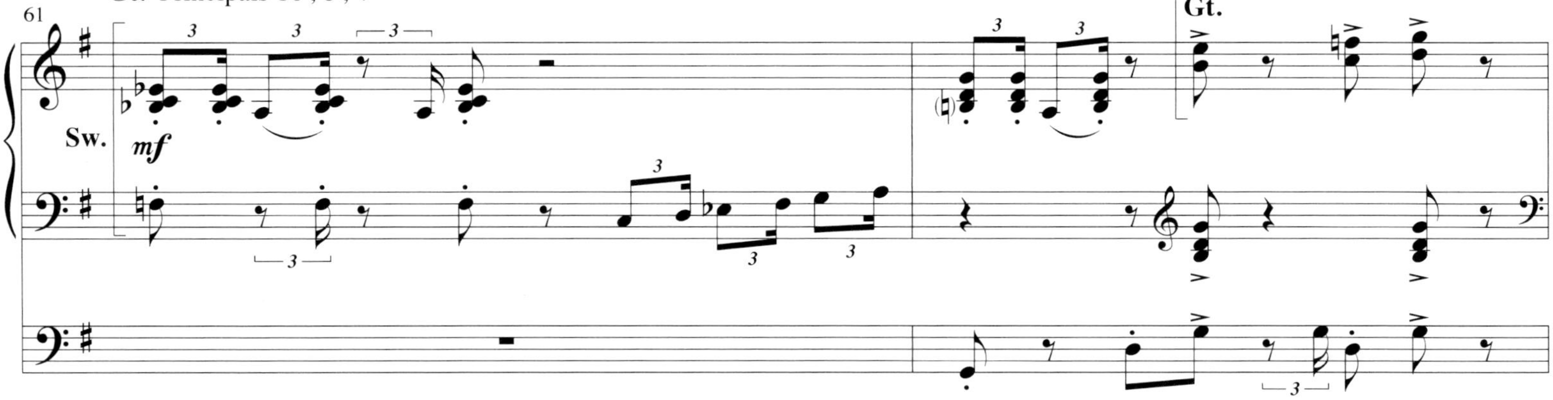

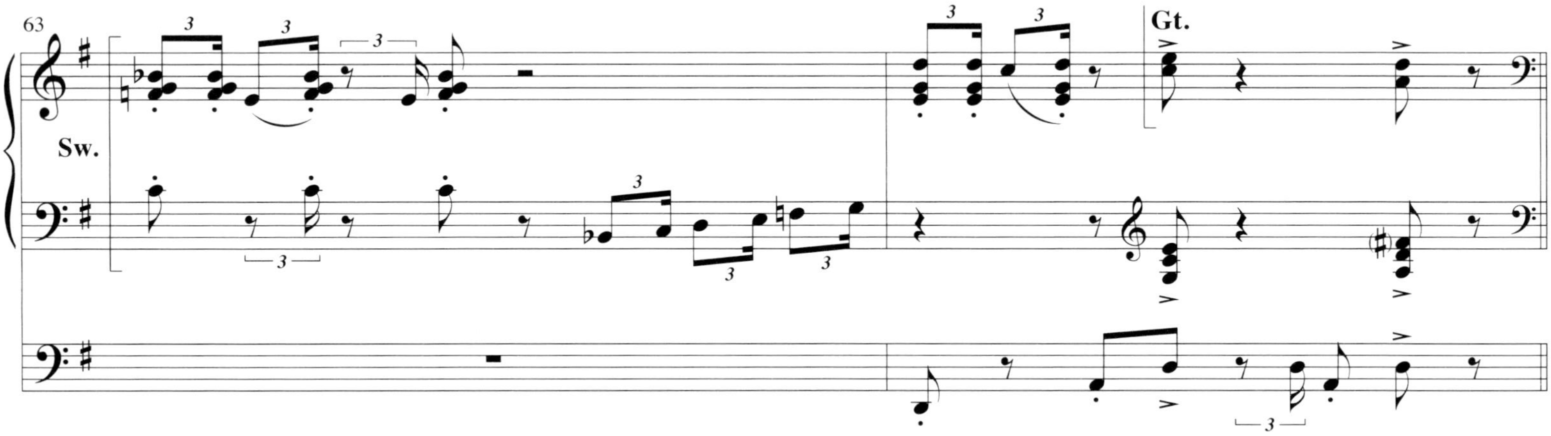

Sw. Bourdon 16'; Principals 8', 4', 2'; Mixture; Trumpet 8' (plus Bassoon 16' and/or Clarion 4')
Gt. Principals 16', 8', 4', 2'; Mixture; Trumpet 8'; **Sw.** to **Gt.** 8'
Ped. Principals 16', 8', 4', 2'; Mixture; **Sw.** to **Ped.** 8'

Ch. Octaves 4', 2'; High Mixture, Trumpet 8' and Schalmey or Regal 4'
Ped. Octaves 4', 2'; High Mixture; **Ch.** to **Ped.** 4'

Sw. Bourdon 16', Octave 4'
Gt. Bourdons 16', 8'; Quint 2⅔'; Octave 2'
Ch. Schalmey or Regal 4' only
Ped. Ch. to **Ped.** 4' only

+ Zimbelstern

Sw. Bourdon 16'; Principals 8', 4', 2'; Mixture; Trumpet 8' (plus Bassoon 16' and/or Clarion 4')
Gt. Principals 16', 8', 4', 2'; Mixture; Trumpet 8'; **Sw.** to **Gt.** 8'
Ped. Principals 32', 16', 8', 4', 2'; Mixture; assertive Reeds 16', 8'; **Sw.** to **Ped.** 8'

Zimbelstern off

78
81
Sw.
Gt.
Full Organ
84
Ped. Full (opt. + Horizontal Trumpet)
86
Ch. Horizontal Trumpet 8'
secco
Sw. Full, Sw. to Sw. 16', 4'
+ Sw. to Gt. 16', 8', 4'
+ Sw. to Ch. 16', 8', 4'
Ch.
fp
molto cresc.
fff
Sw.
Gt.